THE DARK SIDE

Giants
and Ogres

illustrated by David West
and
written by Anita Ganeri

D1315208

PowerKiDS press™
New York

Published in 2011 by The Rosen Publishing Group, Inc.
29 East 21st Street, New York 10010, NY

Designed and produced by
David West Books

Designer: Rob Shone
Editor: Ronne Randall
U.S. Editor: Kara Murray
Illustrator: David West

Photographic credits: 8br/bl, Franklin Township Public Library, New Jersey; 10r, Guatavo Trapp; 11l, Captmondo; 12l/b, jjron; 13, Carol Highsmith; 15t, Flying Pharmacist; 15b, Charles Haynes; 18, Wolfgang Sauber; 20, Bibi Saint-Pol; 22, Roccuz; 22/23, Patrice78500; 23, Alicia Nijdam; 25b, Jingme; 27l, Andrew Bossi; 28t, Michael Haferkamp; 28bl, Christian Bickel.

Library of Congress Cataloging-in-Publication Data

West, David, 1956-
Giants and ogres / illustrated by David West and written by Anita Ganeri. — 1st ed.
p. cm. — (The dark side)
Includes bibliographical references (p.) and index.
ISBN 978-1-61531-898-8 (library binding) — ISBN 978-1-4488-1568-5 (pbk.) — ISBN 978-1-4488-1569-2 (6-pack)
1. Giants—Juvenile literature. 2. Ghouls and ogres—Juvenile literature. I. Ganeri, Anita, 1961- II. Title.
GR560.W47 2011
398.21—dc22

2010006674

Printed in China

CPSIA Compliance Information: Batch #DS0102PK: For Further Information contact Rosen Publishing, New York, New York at 1-800-237-9932

Contents

Introduction

Many bizarre and gruesome creatures roam the world of mythology. Although their origins may be lost in the mists of history, they have preyed on people's superstitions and imaginations since ancient times. Among the most impressive are giants, ogres, and trolls, creatures of enormous size and strength that appear in many of the world's myths and legends. Tales have been told for centuries of their epic battles against each other, humans, and the gods. They are also credited with shaping the landscape and with causing natural disasters, such as earthquakes. Are you ready to go over to the dark side? It will send shivers down your spine . . .

Giants

Crushing all underfoot, a creature taller than a church steeple strides across the countryside. This is the monstrous giant.

A giant is a mythical being of huge size and enormous strength. The English word "giant" comes from the Greek *gigantes*. The Gigantes were a race of giants in Greek mythology (see page 16). Giants are popular foes in myths, legends, folktales, and fairy stories, as are the giant slayers who fight them. No doubt some are based on real-life giants.

King Thrymr, king of the frost giants of Norse mythology, tends his dogs in Jotenheim, home of the giants.

Ruben's painting The Fall of the Titans, *in which the Titans of Greek mythology are overthrown by the Olympian gods.*

Giant Features

Giants take the form of outsize humans, with outsize powers to match—incredible strength, a huge stride, and a booming voice. They often carry outsize weapons. Wooden clubs are a popular choice. Giants can be good or evil, and they can be clever or stupid.

The strength of a giant is illustrated in the fairy tale "The Brave Little Tailor," by the Brothers Grimm. The tailor meets a giant that squeezes water from a boulder! Some real people are giant size and super strong. Among them was Arthur Caley (1837–89), also known as the Middlebush Giant.

It was claimed that Arthur Caley (right) was 7 ft 11 in (2.41 m) tall and weighed 620 lbs (280 kg). He appeared (billed as Colonel Ruth Goshen) in Jack the Giant Killer (poster left).

In "The Brave Little Tailor," the tailor knows he cannot match a giant's strength. To tackle two giants, he throws rocks at them as they sleep. The giants blame one another and defeat each other.

Here is the fire giant Surtr ("the black one"), leader of the fire giants in Norse mythology. He rules Muspelheim with his queen, Sinmara. According to myth, all the fire giants will die at the end of the world.

Heat and fire, in addition to great size and strength, are features of the fire giants of Norse mythology. The fire giants live in Muspelheim, the realm of heat and fire. In Norse myth, it is predicted that the fire giants will destroy the world by setting fire to it.

Pantagruel, a vast giant from the Life of Gargantua and Pantagruel books, sleeps on the shore. He looks enormous compared with the tiny humans in the foreground.

Ancient Giants

Giants appear in many myths and legends from ancient times. Greek and Norse myths tell tales of giants that fought human heroes, as well as each other.

Ancient Greece was home to the Gigantes, the original giants (see page 16), but better known is the Cyclops, the famous one-eyed giant. According to legend, a group of Cyclopses live together on an island. In Homer's *Odyssey*, Odysseus and his men become trapped on the island in the cave of a Cyclops called Polyphemus. The Cyclops eats some of the men, but Odysseus blinds him and manages to escape.

In Greek myth, Atlas is a Titan who fights a battle against Zeus. Zeus punishes Atlas by making him hold up the heavens for eternity.

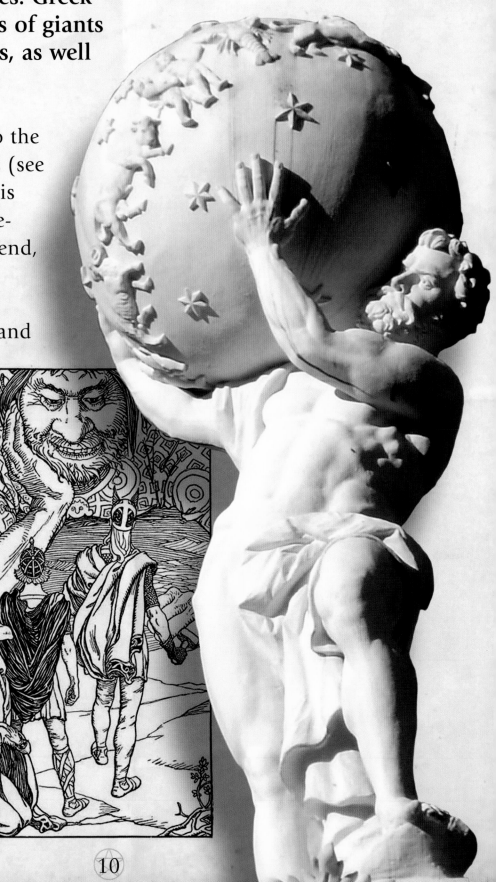

Norse giants are called Jotuns. Here, in the cover picture of the book In the Days of Giants, *the Jotun Skrymir confronts the Norse god Thor.*

To escape from the cave of the Cyclops Polyphemus (right), Odysseus blinds Polyphemus, then slips away underneath the Cyclops's sheep. A carving of Polyphemus (below) shows the single eye in the center of his forehead.

Talos is a giant bronze figure with molten lead for blood. In the story of Jason and the Argonauts, Talos is hypnotized by the sorceress Medea and knocks out the stopper that keeps the lead inside.

Giants in Europe

In European folklore, giants were often said to guard cities, which is why giant figures appear in ceremonial parades and processions. In Britain, giants are often described as stupid and aggressive.

Outside the Guildhall, one of London's grandest buildings, stand two giant wooden figures called Gog and Magog. In British legend, they are Cornish giants, captured by Brutus the Trojan (who is said to have founded London), and forced to serve in the royal palace.

Figures of Gog and Magog in the Royal Arcade, Melbourne, Australia. They are copies of statues in London, where legend says they guard the city.

In German folklore, the giant Rubezahl lives in the Bohemian forest. He is usually kind but sometimes plays tricks. But if he is tricked himself, he flies into a rage.

Celtic myths are packed with giants. The Formorians are a race of giants, believed to be the original inhabitants of Ireland. They are led by Balor of the Evil Eye, whose gaze kills instantly. Most famous of the Celtic giants is Finn McCool.

Irish giant Finn McCool throws a colossal lump of rock at another giant but misses. The rock lands in the sea and becomes the Isle of Man.

In Scottish and Irish folklore, Ogma is a giant and god who takes a huge club into battle.

13

Giants Around the World

Giants of many different kinds come from cultures all over the world, from America in the west to Japan in the east. There are giants the size of mountains, magic giants, gods disguised as giants, and man-eating giants, to name a few.

Mayan myths (the myths of the Mayan people of Mesoamerica) tell of the Cabracan, a destructive mountain-sized giant who creates earthquakes.

The giant Cabracan is killed by the Maya Hero Twins, Hunahpu and Xbalanque. They feed him poisoned birds and bury his enormous body.

Giants from Asia include the bizarre Mikoshi-nyudo from Japan, and Narasimha and Kumbhakarna, who feature in Hindu myths from India. Narasimha is an incarnation of the Hindu god Vishnu. He appears as a giant, half man and half lion. In one story, Narasimha kills Hiranyakashipu, a demon who hates Vishnu for killing his brother. Kumbhakarna is a super-huge, man-eating giant, also from Indian folk stories.

Mikoshi-nyudo is a magical giant encountered on Japanese roads. According to legend, if you try to look up at him, he gets taller. Look up too long and you die!

In the Indian epic tale, the Ramayana, Kumbhakarna is a giant who is always hungry. Here the story is acted out in dance in Bali.

The Hindu god Vishnu in the form of the giant Narasimha tears out the intestines of the demon Hiranyakashipu with his razor-sharp claws.

15

Gods and Giants

In myths and legends, there are many accounts of giants and gods coming to blows. Usually, the giants create chaos, and the gods try to restore order. But many giants are also the offspring of gods, and some are even gods themselves.

The original giants, the Gigantes of Greek mythology, are the sons of Gaea, goddess of the Earth. They fight a battle, the Gigantomachy, with the gods of Mount Olympus and lose as good triumphs over evil.

The fresco, The Fall of the Giants by Giulio Romano, shows the giants being destroyed by a thunderbolt sent by Zeus as they try to storm Mount Olympus.

An illustration from Dante's Inferno, in which Dante and Virgil view the Gigantes and the Titans (both children of Gaea, mother of the Earth) imprisoned in the underworld after their defeat by the gods.

By mistake the Indian giant Kumbhakarna asks for a bed from the god Brahma then falls asleep for six months. He awakes with a terrible hunger and proceeds to eat everything in sight, including quite a few unfortunate humans.

Kumbhakarna (see also page 15) is a truly enormous demonic giant in the Indian epic story, the *Ramayana*. He is killed in battle while fighting with his brother Ravana against the god Rama. The word "hell" comes from Hel, the Norse goddess of death, who is also a giantess. She is mentioned in sagas more than a thousand years old. She rules over the kingdom of the dead, and is described as having a gloomy and sinister appearance.

Hermod, messenger of the gods, bows before the giantess Hel in her kingdom, known as the World of Darkness.

Hero Giants

You might think of giants as terrifying beasts that club and devour people. This is not always the case. A few giants are famous for their great bravery and heroism.

The giant Haymo was defender of the city of Innsbruck and a hero of the Tyrol (an area of Austria). In AD 210, he killed a dragon that was terrifying local people by coming down into the valleys from its mountain lair. Equally brave was the super-strong Greek hero Heracles, famous for achieving twelve near-impossible tasks—the Labors of Hercules.

The Austrian giant Haymo kills a dragon and then cuts out its tongue to prove to the local people that it is dead.

In Greek mythology, a hero is a figure who is somewhere between a human and a god. Orion is one such figure. He is the son of Poseidon (god of the sea), a hunter, and extremely handsome. There are many different stories about his deeds. He hunts animals both on the island of Chios and on Crete, with Artemis, goddess of the hunt. Argus Panoptes, another Greek hero, is a giant with one hundred eyes who kills the monster Echidna.

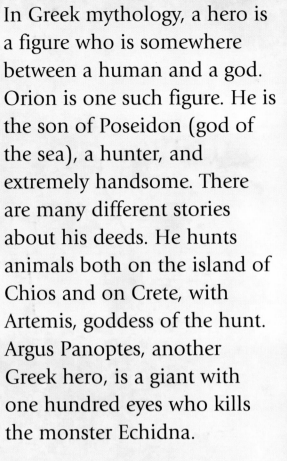

Argus Panoptes, with his hundred eyes, kills Echidna as she sleeps in her cave. Echidna is half nymph, half giant snake, and described as the Mother of all Monsters.

The Greek hero Orion is killed by a giant scorpion and sent by Zeus to live among the stars. The constellation Orion is named after him.

Giant Slayers

Evil and monstrous giants were fair game for heroic warriors. But giant-slaying was not an easy task—cunning and trickery were often needed to defeat a bigger, stronger foe.

Theseus and Heracles were two giant-killers of Greek myth. Theseus met the giant Sinis, who killed travelers by tearing them apart with two bent-over pine trees. Theseus killed Sinis in the same way. Heracles killed the Libyan giant Antaeus, who killed people and kept their skulls.

Theseus (above) kills Sinis by stretching him between two pine trees. Heracles (below) takes away Antaeus's strength by lifting him off the ground then squeezes him to death.

The legendary king of Britain, King Arthur, killed a Spanish giant who had kidnapped his niece Helena and taken her to the French island of Mont Saint-Michel. The most famous giant slayer was David, in the Bible, who became king of Israel. When David was a boy, the Israelite and Philistine armies were at war. The giant Philistine warrior Goliath challenged any Israelite to single combat. David volunteered and killed Goliath with a stone from his sling.

On Mont Saint-Michel, King Arthur dodges the blows of a giant's mighty club before blinding the giant with a swipe of his sword and then killing him.

The biblical story of David and Goliath tells how David knocks down Goliath with a single stone from his sling before cutting off the giant's head.

Land of the Giants

In ancient times, people tried to find ways of explaining peculiar natural features of the landscape (and also vast ancient buildings). Surely only giants had had the size and strength to create them . . .

Huge boulders lying in meadows were one geological feature nobody could explain. In the Basque country of northern Spain, they were said to have been thrown for sport by a race of giants called the Jentilak. "Sleeping giants" are lines of hills that resemble giants stretched out on the ground. Each one has a story that tells us how the giant got there. Giant stones, either standing upright on top of others, or piled into walls, were also explained as the work of giants. In Greece, vast stone walls were called Cyclopean walls, after the giant Cyclops.

The giant Finn McCool is said to have created the Giant's Causeway in Northern Ireland by hurling lumps of earth into the sea.

The Cyclopean walls at Mycenae, a Greek palace complex, were built around 1300 BC. The limestone boulders weigh up to 220 tons (200 t) each.

Northern Ireland boasts the Giant's Causeway, an extraordinary rock formation that stretches out to sea. According to Irish mythology, the giant Finn McCool (see also page 13) created the causeway to allow the Scottish Giant Fingal to reach Ireland. Finn then tricked Fingal, who fled to the island of Staffa.

These rocks in Japan are called the oni-no-sentakuita ("the ogre's washboard") because they look like a huge board for washing clothes.

Could this landscape with its huge boulders, standing stones, and mountain ranges have been shaped by giants?

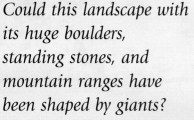

Ogres and Trolls

Three unfortunate humans, their weapons made useless, are captured by a giant figure. It seems that their luck has run out. This giant is an ogre, and he is eager to fill his belly with human flesh.

A Swedish *picture entitled* Ett gammalt bergtroll *("An old mountain troll"). The troll has a typical grumpy face.*

While giants could be good or evil (and sometimes both), the ogres of folklore and fairy tales were always bad! They were cruel and heartless creatures, who devoured humans. Equally bad were the trolls of Scandinavian folklore. They were sometimes giant-sized, sometimes not, and sometimes had magic powers. But they always hated humans. They came down from their mountain homes at night to frighten the local human population.

A character from the 2001 movie Shrek, has become a very famous ogre. Here is an inflatable Shrek in Macy's Thanksgiving Day parade.

Ogres

Giants were terrifying enough, but ogres (and their female counterparts, ogresses) were far worse. Not only were they enormous, superstrong, and mean, but they also ate people.

Ogres first appeared in European literature of the seventeenth century. They were humanlike monsters with big heads, lots of hair, beards, and big bellies. Ogres appear in many fairy tales, including two famous stories by French writer Charles Perrault (1628–1703): "Hop-o'-My-Thumb" and "Puss in Boots."

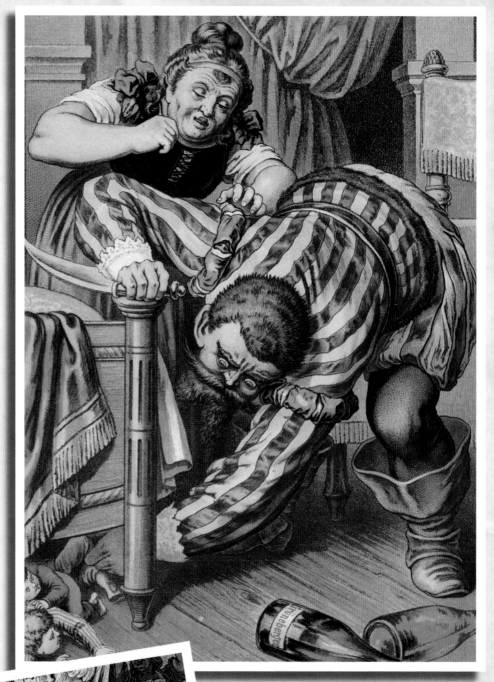

Hop-o'-My-Thumb is one of seven children caught by an ogre. Wary of being killed and eaten, Thumb fools the ogre into killing his own daughters instead. Later, he tricks the ogre out of its fortune.

The hero of "Puss in Boots" is a cat that sets out to make a fortune for his master. Finding a rich ogre who can transform into different creatures, Puss tricks him into turning into a mouse and then eats him.

The Ogre Fountain in Bern, Switzerland shows an ogre sitting on a column devouring a small child. He has more children in his bag. The statue is a popular tourist attraction.

The city of Bern in Switzerland boasts what must be one of the scariest statues in Europe. It is called the Ogre Fountain and was created in 1544. The exact origin of the story is not known. In stories of Yorimitsu, a legendary Japanese soldier who lived around AD 1000, the warrior Watanabe Tsuna fought against an ogress called Ibaragi Oni.

The Japanese warrior Watanabe Tsuna in combat with Ibaragi Oni, an ogress who guards the Rashomon Gate in the city that is now called Kyoto.

Trolls

In early tales from Scandinavian folklore, trolls are giant, ogrelike creatures. But in later stories, trolls are more humanlike and sometimes they are smaller, like elves.

Trolls are squat creatures with long hair on their large heads, and large noses on their craggy faces. But it is not always easy to spot them, because they can shape-shift into other creatures at will. Traditionally, they turn to stone if they are touched by sunlight. In many stories, trolls hide under bridges waiting to pounce on unsuspecting travelers. In the famous folktale "Three Billy Goats Gruff," a bridge-guarding troll is defeated by three goats.

A natural rock formation (above) in a waterfall in Hamarøy, Norway. It is said to be a troll turned to stone when he was caught in sunlight (trolls could also explode in sunlight). A troll (right) lurks under a bridge, watching and waiting for human victims.

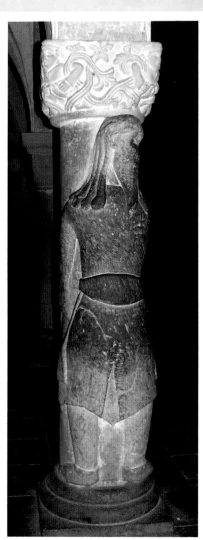

A carving in Lund Cathedral in Sweden is said to be a troll called Fin, who was turned to stone when he threatened to pull down the cathedral by pushing over a pillar.

In disguise, a human-sized troll woman (called a hulder in Norwegian folklore) meets a woodcutter.

Glossary

causeway (KAHZ-way) A raised path or road built across water.

constellation (kon-stuh-LAY-shun) A group of stars in the sky.

foe (FOH) Another word for enemy.

folktales (FOHK-taylz) Stories attached to a particular people or place.

founded (FOWN-did) Built or established, for example, a city.

fresco (FRES-koh) A painting done using watercolors on wet plaster.

geological (jee-uh-LAH-jih-kul) Having to do with the structure of the Earth.

Hindu (HIN-doo) Referring to a culture and religion followed by many people living in or originating from India.

incarnation (in-kar-NAY-shen) The earthly form of a god or goddess.

kidnapped (KID-napt) Taken by force.

lair (LER) A den or cave where a dragon lives.

legends (LEH-jendz) Traditional stories, often based on historical events.

molten (MOHL-ten) Liquid or melted.

mythology (mih-THAH-luh-jee) Traditional stories, not based in historical fact and using supernatural characters to explain human behavior and natural events.

Norse (NAWRS) Describing the people and culture of ancient Scandinavia.

nymph (NIMF) In Greek mythology, a spirit in the form of a beautiful girl.

Olympian (uh-LIM-pee-un) In Greek mythology, referring to a god from Mount Olympus.

sagas (SAH-guz) Very long collections of stories from Norse mythology.

shape-shift (SHAYP-shift) To change form from human to animal, animal to human, or animal to animal.

superstitions (soo-pur-STIH-shunz) Beliefs that things are unlucky.

titans (TY-tunz) Giants of Greek mythology.

Zeus (ZOOS) The king of the gods in Greek mythology.

Further Reading

Berk, Ari. *The Secret History of Giants*. Cambridge, MA: Candlewick Press, 2008.

Ganeri, Anita, and West, David. *An Illustrated Guide to Mythical Creatures*. New York: Hammond, 2009.

Hamilton, John. *Ogres and Giants. Fantasy and Folklore*. Minneapolis: ABDO & Daughters, 2004.

Philip, Neil. *Mythology. DK Eyewitness Books*. New York: DK Children, 2005.

Steffens, Bradley. *Cyclops. Monsters*. San Diego: KidHaven Press, 2005.

A forest troll terrifying a boy

Index

Web Sites

Due to the changing nature of Internet links, PowerKids Press has developed an online list of Web sites related to the subject of this book. This site is updated regularly. Please use this link to access the list:
www.powerkidslinks.com/darkside/giants/